Ohio

Niels R. Jensen

Visit us at
www.abdopublishing.com

Published by ABDO Publishing Company, 8000 West 78th Street, Suite 310, Edina, Minnesota 55439 USA. Copyright ©2010 by Abdo Consulting Group, Inc. International copyrights reserved in all countries. No part of this book may be reproduced in any form without written permission from the publisher. The Checkerboard Library™ is a trademark and logo of ABDO Publishing Company.

Printed in the United States.

Editor: John Hamilton
Graphic Design: Sue Hamilton
Cover Illustration: Neil Klinepier
Cover Photo: iStock Photo

Manufactured with paper containing at least 10% post-consumer waste

Interior Photo Credits: AP Images, Cincinnati Bengals, Cincinnati Reds, Cleveland Browns, Cleveland Cavaliers, Cleveland Indians, Columbus Blue Jackets, Corbis, David Olson, Geoff Mason, Gunter Küchler, Granger Collection, iStock Photo, Jupiterimages, Library of Congress, Mile High Maps, Mountain High Maps, NASA, North Wind Picture Archives, Ohio Historical Society, One Mile Up, Tiffany Komec, U.S. Air Force/Staff Sgt. Bennie Davis III/Major Steve Raspet, and the U.S. Postal Service.
Statistics: State population statistics taken from 2008 U.S. Census Bureau estimates. City and town population statistics taken from July 1, 2007, U.S. Census Bureau estimates. Land and water area statistics taken from 2000 Census, U.S. Census Bureau.

Library of Congress Cataloging-in-Publication Data

Jensen, Niels R., 1949-
  Ohio / Niels R. Jensen.
       p. cm. -- (The United States)
  Includes index.
  ISBN 978-1-60453-670-6
  1. Ohio--Juvenile literature. I. Title.

  F491.3.J46 2010
  977.1--dc22
                         2008052392

Table of Contents

The Buckeye State

Ohio is in the north-central part of the United States. It is part of the Midwest, also called the Heartland. Ohio is one of the top industrial states in the nation. It isn't a big state, but it holds more than 11 million people. It is the seventh-most populous state in the nation.

Ohio's nickname is the Buckeye State because of its many buckeye trees. Early settlers cut down the trees to build cabins.

Today, Ohio is rich with water, soil for farming, and other natural resources. The state is known as a manufacturing center. In recent years, service industries such as health care and education have also become important to Ohio.

Cleveland's Rock and Roll
Hall of Fame and Museum
is one of the most
famous buildings
in the world. It
opened in 1995.

ROCK AND ROLL HALL OF FAME AND MUSEUM

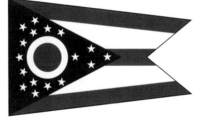

Quick Facts

Name: Ohio is an Iroquoian word meaning "good river." The Native Americans used it to refer to the Ohio River.

State Capital: Columbus

Date of Statehood: March 1, 1803 (17th state)

Population: 11,485,910 (7th-most populous state)

Area (Total Land and Water): 44,825 square miles (116,096 sq km), 34th-largest state

Largest City: Columbus, population 747,755

Nickname: The Buckeye State

Motto: With God All Things Are Possible

State Bird: Cardinal

State Flower: Scarlet Carnation

State Rock: Flint

State Tree: Buckeye

State Song: "Beautiful Ohio"

Highest Point: 1,550 feet (472 m), Campbell Hill

Lowest Point: 455 feet (139 m), Ohio River

Average July Temperature: 73°F (23°C)

Record High Temperature: 113°F (45°C) at Gallipolis, July 21, 1934

Average January Temperature: 28°F (-2°C)

Record Low Temperature: -39°F (-39°C) at Milligan, February 10, 1899

Average Annual Precipitation: 38 inches (97 cm)

Number of U.S. Senators: 2

Number of U.S. Representatives: 18

U.S. Presidents Born in Ohio: Ulysses Grant (1869-1877); Rutherford Hayes (1877-1881); James Garfield (1881); Benjamin Harrison (1889-1893); William McKinley (1897-1901); William Taft (1909-1913); Warren Harding (1921-1923)

U.S. Postal Service Abbreviation: OH

Geography

During the last ice age, one-mile (1.6-km) thick sheets of ice covered two-thirds of Ohio. These glaciers scraped and shaped the land under them. About 14,000 years ago, the last glaciers melted. They left behind deposits of rolling hills and plains in the west and north. Today, this area is good farmland.

Rivers and streams in northern Ohio drain into Lake Erie, and eventually into the Atlantic Ocean. In the southern part of the state, water runs into the Ohio River. From there, water empties into the Mississippi River and eventually the Gulf of Mexico.

Many of Ohio's rivers and streams drain into Lake Erie.

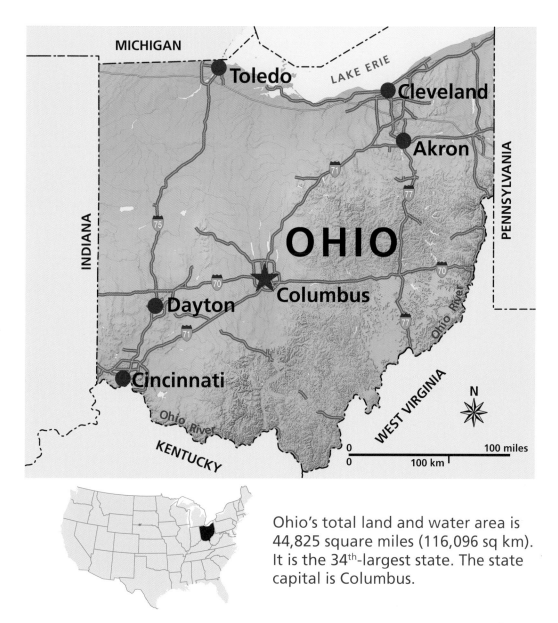

MICHIGAN

Toledo

LAKE ERIE

Cleveland

Akron

PENNSYLVANIA

INDIANA

75

OHIO

71

77

70

70

Dayton

Columbus

71

77

Ohio River

Cincinnati

Ohio River

WEST VIRGINIA

N

KENTUCKY

0   100 miles

0   100 km

Ohio's total land and water area is 44,825 square miles (116,096 sq km). It is the 34th-largest state. The state capital is Columbus.

The Ohio River gave the state its name. The river is about 980 miles (1,577 km) long. Its waters flow to the southwest. The Ohio River is the largest tributary by volume of the Mississippi River. Other major rivers in Ohio include the Cuyahoga, Miami, Maumee, Muskingum, Scioto, and Sandusky Rivers.

Ice-age glaciers did not reach into the southeast part of Ohio. There, you will find the steep ridges and deep valleys of the rugged Appalachian Mountains. The soil is thin and not very good for farming. It is woodland. There are also large deposits of coal.

Ohio has 44,825 square miles (116,096 sq km) total area of land and water. It is the 34th-largest state in the nation. The state's lowest point is 455 feet (139 m) above sea level. It is found in the southwest, where the Ohio River exits the state. Ohio's highest point is Campbell Hill, which stands at 1,550 feet (472 m).

A towboat on the Ohio River pushes barges filled with coal past the city of Cincinnati, Ohio. There are large deposits of coal in the southeastern part of the state.

Climate and Weather

Ohio has a continental climate. Summers are warm and wet. Winters are cold. It is also very cloudy in the winter.

Ohio gets a lot of rain, some thunderstorms, and a few tornadoes. The average yearly precipitation in Ohio is 38 inches (97 cm).

Air masses from Canada and the tropics meet over Ohio. The weather can change swiftly. Lake Erie also affects the weather. As air moves across Lake

A man digs out his car after an Ohio winter storm dumped nearly two feet (.6 m) of snow in the area.

Erie, it often picks up water. The result can be heavy lake effect snow in Ohio's northeastern counties. Some areas get more than 90 inches (229 cm) of snow during winter.

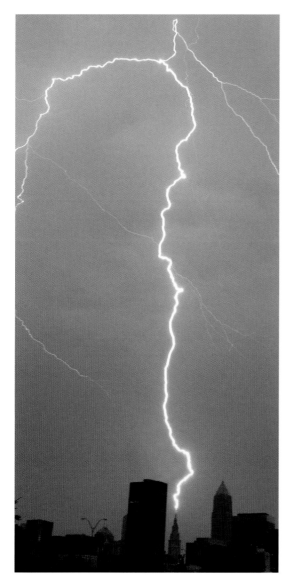

The state's average July temperature is 73 degrees Fahrenheit (23°C). In winter, the average January temperature is 28 degrees Fahrenheit (-2°C). The warmest recorded temperature in the state was 113 degrees Fahrenheit (45°C) at Gallipolis in 1934. The coldest was -39 degrees Fahrenheit (-39°C) at Milligan in 1899.

Lightning strikes a building in downtown Cleveland, Ohio.

Plants and Animals

Ohio has many trees and large forestlands. The Ohio buckeye is the official state tree. When blooming, it has clusters of cream-colored flowers. Ohio also has ash, beech, birch, butternut, cherry, elm, hickory, locust, maple, magnolia, oak, pine, sycamore, and walnut trees.

The white-tailed deer is Ohio's state animal. Foxes, coyotes, groundhogs, opossums, rabbits, beavers, and raccoons live throughout the state. Badgers are rarely seen. There are a few black bears and bobcats.

Ohio's state bird is the cardinal. There are also bluebirds, doves, falcons, herons, kingfishers, larks, mockingbirds, owls, starlings, and woodpeckers. Game birds include ducks, geese, pheasants, and turkeys.

White-Tailed Deer

Red-Tailed Hawk

Groundhogs

Barred Owl

Once nearly extinct in Ohio, bald eagles have made a comeback.

   In 1979, there were only four nesting pairs of bald eagles left in Ohio. Insecticides, used to kill mosquitoes, almost ended the eagle population in Ohio. There are now about 120 nests in 39 counties, and nearly 650 birds.

A dragonfly perches on a stick. Ohio is filled with many interesting insects.

Catfish is a popular food and game fish. There is salmon and sturgeon in Lake Erie. Other local fish include bass, bluegill, carp, crappie, muskellunge, perch, sunfish, trout, and walleye.

Interesting insects include the carpenter ant, backswimmer, dragonfly, damselfly, praying mantis, and walkingstick. There are many butterflies in Ohio. The state also has 60 species of mosquitoes.

History

In the early 1600s, Ohio's Native American tribes lived in villages. They were protected by stockades, and grew corn and vegetables in their gardens. Starting about the year 1650, powerful Iroquois Native Americans from the East attacked. The Iroquois wanted to hunt for beaver in

An Iroquois warrior holding several weapons. He is also wearing snowshoes.

the area. Beaver pelts were prized for hat making in Europe. They could be traded for goods and weapons.

The original tribes were destroyed or pushed out. Few people were left in Ohio. The Iroquois didn't really live here. They mainly came to hunt, and didn't want other people around. In 1670, French explorer René-Robert Cavelier de La Salle probably became the first European to set foot in the Ohio area.

In the late 1600s and early 1700s, French and British explorers came to the Ohio area.

The French and British both wanted the Ohio area. It was a gateway to the riches of the West. That caused the French and Indian War (1754-1763).

A 1787 map shows the Northwest Territory.

The French lost, and Britain got all of the territory. The cost of the war was one cause leading to the American Revolutionary War (1775–1783). After America won its independence from Great Britain, it gained these lands. In 1787, the Northwest Territory was officially formed. Ohio was a part of the Northwest Territory.

On March 1, 1803, Ohio became a state. It was the first state to be admitted from the new Northwest Territory. Ohio became a wealthy farming area, and important cities were built. About 1,000 miles (1,609 km) of canals were dug to transport goods and people.

As a teen, James Garfield (future U.S. president) worked as a hoggee. He drove the horses that pulled barges along the canal. After falling into the canal several times, he got sick. He quit his job and went to college.

In the decades before the American Civil War (1861-1865), thousands of African Americans escaped from slavery through Ohio by the Underground Railroad. The Underground Railroad wasn't a railroad at all. It was a secret network of paths and helpers who led people to freedom.

Many slaves escaped to freedom through Ohio's Underground Railroad.

During the bloody Civil War, Ohio supplied 320,000 troops to the Union North. Thousands of Ohio troops were killed or wounded.

After the war, important industries developed in Ohio. Many new ideas became reality, including the modern airplane. Ohio was the home of Wilbur and Orville Wright. They built the first powered flying machine that could be steered. Their first successful flight was in 1903 in North Carolina.

The Wrights at Huffman Prairie near Dayton, Ohio, in May 1904.

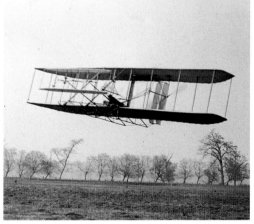

Orville Wright flies over the trees at Huffman Prairie in November 1904.

Did You Know?

- In the early 1800s, John Chapman grew apple orchards in Ohio. He wore strange clothing, walked barefoot, and was a vegetarian. He was friendly with many people. Chapman is better known as Johnny Appleseed. Some of his trees still exist.

- Ohio's statehood was approved on February 19, 1803. But, 150 years later, it was claimed Congress never officially recognized Ohio as a state. To end the debate, President Dwight Eisenhower officially said the state was admitted as of March 1, 1803.

U.S. Brig Niagara

- The United States and Great Britain fought on Lake Erie in the War of 1812. Nine American and six British warships met at Put-in-Bay. The Americans won the battle. Commodore Oliver Perry reported: "We have met the enemy and they are ours." Parts from one of the warships are built into a reconstructed ship that sails the Great Lakes today.

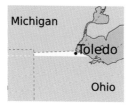

Michigan

Toledo

Ohio

- In 1835, the border between Ohio and Michigan was confusing. Both states claimed the Toledo Strip, and called out their militia. Soldiers went to fight, but luckily did not meet. President Andrew Jackson and Congress stopped the Toledo War. Ohio got Toledo, and Michigan got the Upper Peninsula.

People

Thomas Alva Edison

(1847-1931) was born in Milan, Ohio. His inventions changed the world. They included electric lights, recorded music, and movies. He also built the first electric power station. Edison was one of the most successful inventors of all time, holding 1,093 U.S. patents.

A young Thomas Edison shows off his phonograph in April 1878.

Neil Armstrong (1930-) was the first astronaut to walk on the moon. On July 20, 1969, he stepped onto the surface of the moon and said, "That's one small step for a man, one giant leap for mankind." Armstrong was born in Wapakoneta, Ohio.

John Glenn (1921-) in 1962 became the first American to go around the earth in a spacecraft. From 1974 to 1999, he served as a United States senator from Ohio. In 1998, he became an astronaut again, flying on Space Shuttle *Discovery.*

Steven Spielberg (1946-) is one of the most successful movie directors of all time. Growing up, he filmed his own adventure movies. His first major success was 1975's *Jaws*, about a killer shark. *Jaws*, as well as *E.T. The Extra-Terrestrial*, and *Jurassic Park*, all broke box-office records. Spielberg won Academy Awards for Best Director for *Schindler's List* and *Saving Private Ryan*. Spielberg was born in Cincinnati.

R.L. Stine (1943-) is a bestselling author. Stine was born in Columbus. He began writing when he was nine years old. He graduated from The Ohio State University, and wrote for Scholastic's teen magazine *Bananas*. His first teen horror novel, *Blind Date*, became a bestseller in 1986. His greatest success was his series of *Goosebumps* books.

Annie Oakley (1860-1926) could fire a gun and hit her target almost every time. She had a leading role in *Buffalo Bill's Wild West* show as a sharpshooter. Oakley was one of America's first superstars. In 1894, she starred in Thomas Edison's early Kinetoscope film, *Little Sure Shot.* She was born near Woodland, Ohio.

Granville Woods (1856-1910) was one of the greatest inventors of his time. His inventions included an automatic railroad brake and a telegraph that worked on a moving train. Woods was born in Columbus.

Cities

Columbus is the capital of Ohio. It is also the state's largest city, with a population of about 747,755. Many people in Columbus work in government jobs. Other Columbus industries include insurance, banking, retail, and technology. The Ohio State University at Columbus is one of the largest campuses in the nation. It has about 52,000 students.

Cleveland is on the southern shore of Lake Erie. Its population is about 438,042. In the early 1800s, a canal connected Cleveland to the Ohio River. Railways and roads were built. The city became a major manufacturing center and steel producer. Today, Cleveland includes many theaters, colleges, and museums. It is also home to the Rock and Roll Hall of Fame and Museum.

The Rock and Roll Hall of Fame and Museum (left) overlooks Lake Erie.

Cincinnati is located on the shores of the Ohio River. It has a population of about 332,458. Several big businesses have their headquarters here, including Procter & Gamble, the maker of Ivory Soap. The University of Cincinnati is also located here.

Toledo is at the west end of Lake Erie. It is a busy shipping hub, with a population of about 295,029. The city is known for making glass, car parts, and Jeeps. There are also health care facilities, retail centers, and colleges, including the University of Toledo.

Akron owes its development to a canal that linked Lake Erie with the Ohio River. Industries built many manufacturing plants here. The city is the home of the Goodyear Tire and Rubber Company. The University of Akron is also located here. Akron's population is about 207,934.

Dayton has a population of about 155,461. It was from Dayton that the Wright Brothers pioneered the building of airplanes. Today, Dayton companies continue to conduct aerospace, engineering, and technology research. The city is also the home of Huffy Bicycle Company.

Transportation

About 1,000 miles (1,609 km) of canals once connected Lake Erie with the Ohio River. That made it possible to transport goods and

Tugboats on the Ohio River.

passengers to the Mississippi River. It was also useful for sending the state's farm products to market.

The canals were eventually replaced with railways. Today, trains still move passengers and freight between the Midwest and the East Coast.

Modern roads, highways, and interstates were built in the 20th century. The busy interstates of I-70, I-71, I-75, I-77, I-80, and I-90 run through Ohio.

Cleveland's airport is a hub, or home base, for Continental Airlines. Cincinnati's airport is a hub for Delta Airlines. There are other major airports at Akron-Canton, Columbus, Dayton, and Toledo.

The Cleveland Hopkins Airport is a hub for Continental Airlines.

Natural Resources

Food and agricultural is a $79 billion industry in Ohio. The state has more than 77,000 farms. The best farmland is in Ohio's northwestern half. Major agricultural products include Swiss cheese, eggs, corn, tomatoes, soybeans, and grain. The state's farmers also raise many hogs, sheep, dairy cattle, and turkeys.

The state's hilly eastern and southern regions have hardwood forests. Oak and walnut trees are used in the furniture and paper industries.

Coal has been mined in Ohio's Appalachian region since 1800. The state has one of the largest coalfields in the country. Ohio produces more than 25 million tons (22.7 million metric tons) of coal per year.

One of the largest free-range turkey farms in Ohio is in New Carlisle. On a free-range farm, the animals run free. They are not kept in pens.

A farmer hauls a wagon full of sweet corn back to his barn in Peninsula, Ohio.

Industry

   Ohio is a leading producer of steel and machinery. It is the nation's second-largest maker of cars, trucks, and car parts. It also makes chemicals, glass, matches, paint, refrigerators, soap, and many other products.

   More than 1,000 manufacturing plants produce plastic parts, rubber, and tires. Many are in the Akron area.

The Goodyear Tire & Rubber Company of Akron, Ohio, has been making tires since 1898.

NASA's John H. Glenn Research Center is in Cleveland, Ohio.

There is a large aerospace and defense contracting industry in the state. Ohio companies make airplanes, missiles, space vehicles, tanks, engines, and aircraft parts. NASA's Glenn Center near Cleveland and Wright-Patterson Air Force Base near Dayton are major research facilities.

Tourism is a $38 billion business in Ohio. There are many cultural and historical sites, plus outdoor activities to explore.

Sports

Ohio has many professional sports teams. The Cincinnati Reds are a Major League Baseball National League team. The Cleveland Indians play baseball in the American League. The Cincinnati Bengals and Cleveland Browns both play in the National Football League. The Cleveland Cavaliers are in the National Basketball Association. The Columbus Blue Jackets play in the National Hockey League.

The state's great outdoors offers many opportunities for camping, biking, hiking, hunting, and rock climbing. There are more than 70 state parks.

Ohio has many rivers, streams, and lakes. Boating and fishing are very popular.

The state also has much to offer in the wintertime. Outdoor activities include cross-country skiing, snowmobiling, ice fishing, skating, and iceboating.

An iceboat racer from Toledo, Ohio, waits to compete.

Entertainment

Ohio has more than 100 art museums and galleries. There are many theaters and orchestras. The Rock and Roll Hall of Fame and Museum is in Cleveland. It is dedicated to the singers, songwriters, musicians, and others in the music industry. Ohio also has other hall-of-fame organizations. They include the Pro Football Hall of Fame in Canton, and the National Inventors Hall of Fame Museum in Akron.

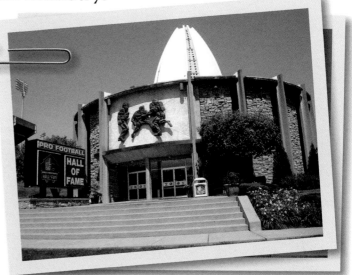

The Pro Football Hall of Fame opened in September 1963.

The National Museum of the United States Air Force includes Warrior Airman exhibits.

The National Museum of the United States Air Force is located at the Wright-Patterson Air Force Base near Dayton. It exhibits more than 400 airplanes.

Kings Island and Cedar Point are popular amusement parks. There are hundreds of festivals, fairs, and shows, including a Renaissance festival. Cincinnati, Cleveland, Columbus, and Toledo all have major zoological gardens.

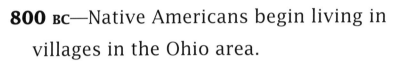

Timeline

800 BC—Native Americans begin living in villages in the Ohio area.

1650—The Iroquois enter the Ohio area, hunting for beaver pelts.

1670—French explorer René-Robert Cavelier de La Salle enters the Ohio area.

1754-1763—Conflict over Ohio is one cause of the French and Indian War.

1783—The United States is awarded the Northwest Territories, including Ohio, from Great Britain.

1800—Coal mining begins in Ohio.

1803—Ohio becomes the 17th state.

1832—The first canal between Lake Erie and the Ohio River opens.

1835—Ohio and Michigan argue over their border. It is known as the Toledo War.

1861—American Civil War begins. Ohio troops fight for the Union North.

1995—The Rock & Roll Hall of Fame and Museum opens in Cleveland, Ohio.

2008—A blizzard strikes Ohio, closing roads and airports. Columbus receives a record-setting 20 inches (51 cm) of snow.

Glossary

Canal—A canal is a waterway built to carry freight and people in boats. Canals often connect lakes and rivers.

Glacier—Glaciers are immense layers of ice that grow and shrink when the climates change. They change the land beneath them.

Insecticides—Chemicals used to kill mosquitoes and other insects. The insecticide DDT was used in the United States from the 1940s until it was banned in 1972. DDT is poisonous to people and animals. The chemical nearly wiped out all the bald eagles in Ohio.

Iroquois—The Iroquois were a powerful Native American group. Member tribes included the Cayuga, Mohawk, Oneida, Onondaga, Seneca, and Tuscarora.

Kinetoscope—An early form of movie projector designed for one person at a time to view a film. It was invented by

Thomas Edison and his employee William Dickson from 1888 to 1892. The name is a combination of Greek words: *Kineto,* meaning "movement," and *scopos,* meaning "to view."

Lake Effect Snow—Wintertime weather systems pick up moisture over large bodies of water, such as Lake Erie. It then falls as deep snow once it comes ashore.

Militia—Military units of citizen-soldiers, unlike the regular Army. The National Guard is a militia.

Patent—The legal right, as issued by a government, for an inventor to make, use, and sell a specific product.

Tributary—A river or stream that flows into a larger river or lake. For example, the Ohio River flows into the Mississippi River. Therefore, the Ohio River is a tributary of the Mississippi River.

Underground Railroad—People who were against slavery created the Underground Railroad to help African Americans escape from the Southern slave states. It was a secret network of safe houses and connecting routes.

Index

More people live in Chicago than any other city in Illinois or the entire Midwest.

ILLINOIS

Name: Illinois is the French spelling of an American Indian tribe called the Illiniwek.

State Capital: Springfield, population 117,090

Date of Statehood: December 3, 1818 (21st state)

Population: 12,901,563 (5th-most populous state)

Area (Total Land and Water): 57,914 square miles (149,997 sq km), 25th-largest state

Largest City: Chicago, population 2,836,658

Nicknames: The Prairie State or the Land of Lincoln

Motto: State Sovereignty, National Union

State Bird: Cardinal

State Flower: Violet

State Mineral: Flourite

State Tree: White Oak

State Song: "Illinois"

Highest Point: Charles Mound, 1,235 feet (376 m)

Lowest Point: Mississippi River, 279 feet (85 m)

Average July Temperature: 75°F (24°C)

Record High Temperature: 117°F (47°C), East St. Louis, July 14, 1954

Average January Temperature: 25°F (-4°C)

Record Low Temperature: -36°F (-38°C), Congerville, January 5, 1999

Average Annual Precipitation: 39 inches (99 cm)

Number of U.S. Senators: 2

Number of U.S. Representatives: 19

U.S. Presidents Born in Illinois: Ronald Reagan

U.S. Postal Service Abbreviation: IL

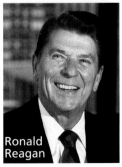

Ronald Reagan

Geography

Illinois is in the Mississippi Valley region of the Midwestern United States. It is the 25th-largest state. Illinois spreads across 57,914 square miles (149,997 sq km). Its map shape is almost rectangular. The state is much longer north to south than it is wide from east to west.

To the north of Illinois is Wisconsin. Its western neighbors are Missouri and Iowa . On the south lies Kentucky. Across its eastern line is Indiana. The northeast border of Illinois juts out into Lake Michigan.

Most of Illinois is a flat plain. Its average elevation is about 600 feet (183 m) above sea level. The central part of the state is a region with very good soil for farming. The northern one-third of Illinois is an urban region.

WISCONSIN

Rockford

IOWA

Rock River

90

Chicago

LAKE MICHIGAN

88

Joliet

80

74

39

Peoria

57

ILLINOIS

INDIANA

Illinois River

74

72

★

Springfield

70

Mississippi River

55

70

N

100 miles

0

0

100 km

MISSOURI

64

Wabash River

57

24

Ohio River

KENTUCKY

Illinois's total land and water area is 57,914 square miles (149,997 sq km). It is the 25th-largest state. The state capital is Springfield.

The hilliest part of the state is found in the northwest corner. The highest point in Illinois is Charles Mound. It is 1,235 feet (376 m) above sea level. Smaller and rounder hills are found in the southern third of the state. The hills become less round the closer they are to the border with Kentucky. The lowest point in Illinois is in the southern region. It is on the Mississippi River. There, the elevation is 279 feet (85 m) above sea level.

The Mississippi River is one of Illinois's most important waterways. Others include the Wabash, Ohio, Chicago, Rock, Kankakee, Calumet, and Illinois Rivers. There are about 275 important rivers and streams in Illinois. The state's largest inland body of water is man-made Carlyle Lake.

The Ohio River and the Mississippi River come together at Cairo, Illinois.

Climate and Weather

Illinois has hot summers and cold winters. The southern part of the state is usually warmer for more months of the year than the northern part and has milder winters. That is because the state stretches the long distance of 400 miles (644 km) from north to south.

The hottest month in every part of the state is July. The statewide average temperature during July is 75°F (24°C). The hottest day on record in Illinois was July 14, 1954, when the temperature climbed to 117°F (47°C) in the city of East St. Louis.

Illinois winters are cold and snowy.

Illinois's coldest month is January. Temperatures average 25°F (-4°C) for the entire state. January 5, 1999, was the coldest it ever has been in Illinois. The temperature on that day in the city of Congerville was -36°F (-38°C).

Illinois receives an average of 39 inches (99 cm) of rain and snow during a normal year. Thunderstorms and hailstorms are common. Tornados and blizzards also occur sometimes.

A tornado moved along the ground near Granville, Illinois, in 2004.

Plants and Animals

White Oak

More than 70 types of trees are native to Illinois. Among them are hickory, maple, elder, elm, beech, ash, sycamore, walnut, cottonwood, willow, and pine. White oak is the state's official tree. It is prized for its strong and long-lasting wood. It is used in the making of barrels, furniture, and ships.

The state's native wild flowers come in many different varieties. Some of these are shooting star, bluebell, coneflower, daisy, goldenrod, aster, lilac, morning glory, prairie rose, spiderwort, sunflower, and lily. The state's official flower is the violet.

Wildflowers on
an Illinois prairie.

Spiderwort

Shooting Star

Barn Owl
in Violets

The official animal of Illinois is the white-tailed deer. Also plentiful are shrews, armadillos, skunks, chipmunks, gophers, opossums, minks, raccoons, muskrats, bats, badgers, weasels, rabbits, squirrels, mice, beavers, bobcats, foxes, moles, voles, coyotes, and river otters.

The birds of Illinois include bluebirds, larks, bobwhites, woodpeckers, magpies, chickadees, wrens, finches, goshawks, owls, golden eagles, plovers, seagulls, pelicans, herons, sandpipers, terns, loons, and grebes. The cardinal is the official bird of Illinois.

A few of the many types of fish that can be found in Illinois are carp, catfish, crappie, salmon, gar, darter, perch, paddlefish, shiner, herring, and bowfin. Illinois chose the bluegill to be its official state fish. Bluegill is a member of the sunfish family. It lives in rivers and streams.

A bluegill.

The white-tailed deer is the official animal of Illinois.

Badger

Weasel

Bobwhites

History

The first people to settle in Illinois were called the Mound Builders. They came thousands of years ago and then disappeared around 1500 AD. Their lands were taken over by six Native American tribes who called themselves the Illiniwek. Almost all of them were killed during an invasion by Iroquois tribes in the late 1600s.

A missionary and a fur trader from France were the first Europeans to explore Illinois. They were Father Jacques Marquette and Louis Joliet. They paddled in canoes down the Mississippi River and then back north along the Illinois River in 1673. In 1680, France built its first Illinois fort near what is today the city of Peoria. In 1699, the French built a town near today's city of Cahokia.

Father Marquette holds up a symbol of peace to Native Americans.

A war that started in 1754 between France and Great Britain ended nine years later with

Early French settlers enjoy themselves in Illinois.

France losing. The French gave Illinois to Great Britain. Britain then handed it over to the young United States at the end of America's Revolutionary War in 1783.

In those days, Illinois was part of what was called the Northwest Territory. The Northwest Territory included the future states of Illinois, Ohio, Indiana, Michigan, Wisconsin, and a part of Minnesota.

The territory was divided several times during the early 1800s. Illinois Territory was formed in 1809. It was granted statehood on December 3, 1818. It was the 21ˢᵗ state admitted to the Union.

A canal boat at Lockport, Illinois, in 1900.

A Chicago & Northwestern passenger train in 1899.

Canals were dug and railroads built across Illinois in the decades after statehood. These improvements made it easy to move natural resources and finished products around the state. As a result, Illinois became a very attractive place to many companies. The state soon became a leading source of just about everything the rest of the nation needed to grow bigger and better.

General Grant   General Lee

Abraham Lincoln was the 16th president of the United States.

The Civil War ended with General Lee's surrender to General Grant.

Illinois's most famous citizen of the mid-1800s was Abraham Lincoln. His election as president of the United States in 1860 led to the Civil War. Lincoln had come to office promising to end slavery in the states of the South.

The people of the South used their armies to resist Lincoln. The war ended in 1865 with the defeat of the South and the slaves set free.

Illinois industrialized rapidly after the Civil War. More railroads were built. Many of them led straight to the port city of Chicago. They brought cattle, wheat, and corn from farms out West and elsewhere. Very quickly, Illinois became the nation's largest market for beef and grain. Chicago and other major Illinois cities attracted people from all over the country and the globe. The industrial and economic might of Illinois helped make it the second-most important state during the first half of the 1900s.

Illinois became an even more important center of transportation and commerce during the second half of the 1900s and at the dawn of the 2000s. Today, Illinois has its eyes set on a future filled with greater dreams and brighter hopes.

Did You Know?

- Illinois is so flat that the state's tallest point is actually a building. It is the Sears Tower in the city of Chicago. The skyscraper rises 1,450 feet (442 m) above the ground. If you add the elevation of the ground it stands on, the top of the Sears Tower is at an elevation of 2,030 feet (619 m) above sea level.

- The world's first McDonald's restaurant opened in the city of Des Plaines, Illinois, in 1955. The world's first Dairy Queen opened 15 years earlier in the city of Joliet.

- Cracker Jack is a snack that kids love as much today as when it was invented. The world got its first taste of Cracker Jack at the 1893 Chicago World's Fair.

- The city of Morton is known as the pumpkin capital of the world. Eighty percent of the world's supply of canned pumpkins comes from this Illinois city.

- The world's tallest man was from Illinois. Robert Wadlow stood nearly 9 feet (3 m) tall and weighed almost 500 pounds (227 kg).

People

Barack Obama (1961–) became a United States senator from Illinois in 2005. On November 4, 2008, he was elected 44th president of the United States. He gave his victory speech in Chicago's Grant Park. On January 20, 2009, he was sworn in as president in Washington, D.C.

Obama was born and grew up in Hawaii. He graduated from Columbia University in New York and Harvard Law School in Massachusetts. He became the first African American president of the *Harvard Law Review*, a student-run journal. After graduation, he moved to Chicago, Illinois, where he worked to help people who had lost their jobs.

Ronald Reagan (1911-2004) was the 40th president of the United States, serving from 1981 to 1989. Earlier, Reagan was the governor of California from 1967 to 1975. Before that, he was a popular actor who starred in many Hollywood films of the 1930s, 1940s, and 1950s. Reagan was born in Tampico, Illinois.

Abraham Lincoln (1809-1865) was the 16th president of the United States, serving from 1861 to 1865. Lincoln ended slavery in the United States. He began his career in politics in Illinois. He became a lawyer after that. Voters then sent him to Congress. Lincoln later spent several years helping create the Republican Party. He was born in Kentucky. He moved to Illinois when he was 21. Lincoln's life was ended by a killer's bullet.

Oprah Winfrey (1954-) is one of the most famous talk show hosts in the world. *The Oprah Winfrey Show* has been produced in Chicago, Illinois, since 1986. She has won or been nominated for many entertainment awards. In addition, she has been honored for her work helping people around the world. Winfrey was named one of the 100 Most Influential People of the 20th Century by *Time* magazine. She was born in Mississippi.

Walt Disney (1901-1966) was a famous cartoonist and theme park designer. Mickey Mouse and Donald Duck were creations of the cartoon studio founded by Disney in the 1920s. He won a record 26 Oscar awards. Disney also was the designer of the Disneyland and Disney World theme parks. He was born in Chicago.

Richard Sears (1863-1914) was a founder of the department store chain that today bears his name. The company started in the early 1890s. It quickly became very popular with people who lived too far from cities where all the best stores were located. Sears made it possible for farm families and others to easily buy the things they wanted. All they had to do was order from his catalog and their purchases would be shipped directly to their homes. Sears was born in Stewartville, Minnesota, but built his company in Chicago.

A Sears store in Chicago.

Cities

Chicago is the Windy City.

Chicago has more people living in it than any other Illinois city. Its population is 2,836,658. That also makes it the third-biggest city in the nation.

Chicago's nickname is the Windy City because of the strong winds that blow from nearby Lake Michigan. Those same winds helped fan a fire in 1871 that burned much of the city to the ground.

Chicago was founded in 1833. It did not take long for the city to become the Midwest's most important link to the business markets of the eastern United States and Europe. Today, Chicago is also a center of business, education, science, entertainment, and politics. Several of the tallest buildings in the world are in Chicago.

Manufacturing was once the most important activity in **Rockford**. Today, high technology companies are very important in the city. Rockford is located in the middle of the most northern part of the state. Rockford's population is 156,596. It is the state's third-largest city.

Joliet is located about 40 miles (64 km) southwest of Chicago. It is one of the fastest growing cities in

Illinois. Its population is 144,316. Many people enjoy Joliet's historical and artistic attractions, as well as NASCAR racing, baseball, and other sporting events.

The capital city of Illinois is **Springfield**. The city's population is 117,090. Springfield was Abraham Lincoln's home for nearly 25 years before he became president of the United States. Lincoln is buried in Springfield. The city was founded in 1821.

Many people visit Abraham Lincoln's tomb in Springfield, Illinois. Lincoln's wife, Mary, and three of their four sons are also buried here.

Peoria is located close to the very center of the state, in the heart of farm country. Its population is 113,546. The city was first settled in 1680, but it did not become a city until 1835. The city's motto is "Will It Play in Peoria?" That means the people of America will probably like a new product or idea if the people of Peoria like it first.

Transportation

Illinois is one of America's most important states when it comes to transportation. Its central location and good systems for moving people and products make it so.

Most of the nation's major freight and passenger railroads connect in Illinois. There are approximately 10,000 miles (16,093 km) of tracks in the state.

A train station in Chicago, Illinois. Trains transport people and freight across the state and across the country.

Many major interstate highways also meet in Illinois. The state has nearly 140,000 miles (225,308 km) of roads.

Each year, more than 26 million tons (24 million metric tons) of natural resources and finished products pass through the Port of Chicago. Ships and barges leaving the port can reach either the Atlantic Ocean or the Gulf of Mexico.

O'Hare International Airport is located just outside Chicago. About 70 million people fly in and out of O'Hare each year. More than 2,400 planes take off and land there every day. Illinois is also served by nine other major airports.

Chicago's O'Hare International Airport is one of the busiest airports in the country.

Natural Resources

Three-quarters of the land in Illinois is used for raising crops. Corn brings the most money to the state. Soybeans are also important. Illinois is the nation's second-largest exporter of grains that will be turned into food for animals.

A barn sits in an Illinois farm field surrounded by corn and soy beans, two import crops grown in the state. Wind turbines have been placed in many Illinois farm fields. The power generated helps cities across the state.

Illinois ranks 36th among the 50 states for number of trees harvested from forests. A big reason why it does not rank higher is that only about 10 percent of Illinois is covered with forests.

Beneath the ground of Illinois lie huge deposits of coal and much smaller amounts of petroleum. Illinois leads the nation in production of industrial sand and gravel. Large amounts of crushed stone are used in construction projects.

Coal mining in Saline County, Illinois.

A gravel pit in Clinton County, Illinois.

Industry

The state of Illinois produces many important products. These include machinery, plastics, transportation equipment, computer hardware and software, and electronics. Illinois factories earn the most money by manufacturing chemicals. Those chemicals then are used to make other things. For example, one company in Illinois produces chemicals that are used to make medicines, cosmetics, and foods.

Illinois is a major center for financial services. These include banks, insurance companies, and investment brokers. Illinois is home to one of the nation's most important commodity markets.

Brokers at work in the Chicago Mercantile Exchange.

This commodity market is called the Chicago Mercantile Exchange. People buy and sell contracts for huge amounts of grain, meat, lumber, textiles, metals, energy, and other basic resources known as commodities. This buying and selling helps set the price for the foods you eat and the clothes you wear.

Sports

Illinois has six major league sports teams. It also has many other professional sports teams.

The place in Illinois where the most sports action occurs is Chicago. Fans there can enjoy Major League Baseball with either the Cubs or the White Sox. They can enjoy football with the Chicago Bears. They can go to a basketball game and see the Chicago Bulls play. Or they can watch the Blackhawks of the National Hockey League. Soccer fans have the Chicago Fire.

Other places in Illinois offer plenty of great sports. Joliet has a minor league baseball team and a NASCAR speedway. In the east-central part of the state is the University of Illinois at Urbana-Champaign, which hosts powerful football and basketball teams.

University of Illinois fans cheer their football team, the Fighting Illini.

Entertainment

Bright lights and excitement are found on almost every street of downtown Chicago's Loop District. There are performances by top ballet and dance troupes, theatrical companies, orchestras, and musicians of every type. Chicago is especially famous for its comedy clubs and art showcases.

People who like the outdoors can choose from more than 60 state parks, forests, and major recreation spots to hike, camp, swim, ride horses, go boating, and more.

Many people enjoy libraries and museums. The ones in Illinois are among the very best in the nation. Chicago's Field Museum is a national treasure, with many amazing science and history exhibits. Among them is the world's largest and most complete *Tyrannosaurus rex* skeleton.

Chicago's Field Museum has a number of amazing exhibits. Visitors come to see the world's largest and most complete *T-rex* fossil, named Sue.

Timeline

Fort Massac

1500s—Illiniwek Native Americans arrive.

1673—France explores Illinois.

1699—France begins to build forts and towns in Illinois.

1763—Great Britain controls Illinois.

1783—Britain surrenders Illinois to the United States.

1818—Illinois becomes the 21st state.

1820s—Illinois begins building canals.

1850s—Illinois becomes the Midwest's most important hub of transportation.

1861-65—Illinois fights in the Civil War on the side of its most famous citizen, President Abraham Lincoln.

1890s—Illinois becomes the biggest supplier of grains and beef to markets of the eastern United States.

1933—The World's Fair is held in Chicago.

1993—The Mississippi River floods many homes and businesses.

2009—Former Illinois Senator Barack Obama is sworn in as the 44th president of the United States.

Glossary

Canal—A man-made river deep and wide enough for boat traffic. Canals are often shortcuts between cities or countries. People and cargo traveling on boats using canals can travel in less time than might otherwise be possible.

Civil War—The war fought between America's Northern and Southern states from 1861-1865. The Southern states were for slavery. They wanted to start their own country. Northern states fought against slavery and a division of the country.

Fur Trader—A person who buys and sells the soft, thick coat of hair taken from certain animals. The fur is later made into warm clothing. Beavers and minks are examples of animals from which the fur is taken.

Industrialize—To change a society from one in which work is done mainly by hand to one in which work is done mainly by machines.

NASCAR—National Association for Stock Car Auto Racing. A popular sporting event with races held across the United States. The Chicagoland Speedway in Joliet, Illinois, hosts many NASCAR races.

Oscar—A gold statue awarded to the year's best movie actors, writers, directors, producers, and technicians by the Academy of Motion Picture Arts and Sciences. It is also known as an Academy Award. About 40 Oscars are made each year by the manufacturer in Chicago, Illinois.

Prairie—A large area of level or mostly level grassland.

Revolutionary War—The war fought between the American colonies and Great Britain from 1775-1783. It is also known as the War of Independence and the American Revolution.

Transportation—The way that people and products are moved from one place to another.

Urban—Referring to a city or city life.

Index

The Prairie State

Illinois is a state in America's Midwest. It has two nicknames. One is the Prairie State. The other is the Land of Lincoln. Illinois is where President Abraham Lincoln spent most of his adult life.

Many people live in Illinois. It is the Midwest's most populated state.

Most of Illinois is flat as far as the eye can see. But there are places where hills rise, winding rivers flow, and majestic forests appear.

Illinois is as famous for its farms as it is for its many types of manufacturing, service, and financial companies. But the state is most famous as a center of transportation. Much of what the Midwest produces and uses passes through Illinois on its journey to people's homes, offices, and schools.

Table of Contents

Visit us at
www.abdopublishing.com

Published by ABDO Publishing Company, 8000 West 78th Street, Suite 310, Edina, Minnesota 55439 USA. Copyright ©2010 by Abdo Consulting Group, Inc. International copyrights reserved in all countries. No part of this book may be reproduced in any form without written permission from the publisher. The Checkerboard Library™ is a trademark and logo of ABDO Publishing Company.

Printed in the United States.

Editor: John Hamilton
Graphic Design: Sue Hamilton
Cover Illustration: Neil Klinepier
Cover Photo: iStock Photo

Manufactured with paper containing at least 10% post-consumer waste

Interior Photo Credits: AirPhoto/Jim Wark, Alamy, AP Images, Chicago Bears, Chicago Blackhawks, Chicago Bulls, Chicago Cubs, Chicago Fire, Chicago White Sox, Comstock, Corbis, David Olson, Getty, Granger Collection, Gunter Küchler, iStock Photo, Library of Congress, McDonald's, Mile High Maps, Mountain High Maps, North Wind Picture Archives, One Mile Up, Sears, U.S. Navy, and Universal Pictures.
Statistics: State population statistics taken from 2008 U.S. Census Bureau estimates. City and town population statistics taken from July 1, 2007, U.S. Census Bureau estimates. Land and water area statistics taken from 2000 Census, U.S. Census Bureau.

Library of Congress Cataloging-in-Publication Data

Smith, Rich, 1954-
 Illinois / Rich Smith.
    p. cm. -- (The United States)
 Includes index.
 ISBN 978-1-60453-648-5
 1. Illinois--Juvenile literature. I. Title.

 F541.3.S64 2010
 977.3--dc22

                        2008051042

Illinois

Rich Smith